Wildflowers

the first collection

written by k.e. | *cover by* kinsey olson

Wildflowers

ISBN-13: 978-1530900473
ISBN-10: 1530900476

Cover by Kinsey Olson, Bristle Designs
For inquiries, contact kinseyleeolson@gmail.com | @kinseyolson

To my father,
my last star on the left,
keep sending me the laughter and joy and love.

This book is for you, and I hope you will see that these words were never mine to keep, but yours to find. I have been writing these words for you all along. Through the pain and love, the valleys and peaks.

So I hope they make you happy, make you cry, make you angry, make you *feel*. But most of all, I hope they remind you that you are not alone. In suffering and in joy, you are not alone.

Oh, and this title is probably deceiving. I had hopes that all my words would be soft and gentle and kind, but my words knew better. They knew that truth is often painful, broken, and a little angry.

But wildflowers, for me, stand for something spectacular. Look at them! Wherever their roots can be, they *grow, grow, grow*. I want to be that. I want to be torn down by life and have my seeds and roots, my soul and body, still trusting enough to find home again. I want that kind of wild running through my veins.

So maybe the title is good. Maybe the wildflowers understand it more than any of us.

We must rebuild.

I just want you to remember something, remember that life is pretty dang hard, and trying to navigate against those odds is a tough task. So be good to yourself, love yourself like crazy, and take every single thing that life gives you – good and not so good. It is all a part of it, and it is all a part of your story, of you.

So here is to love, and growing, and loss, and hope.

P.S. *None of these words are complete, and well, that is just how it goes sometimes; you will find that some of these pages have no ending, and if you come upon one you feel unfinished, know that it was always meant for you... and finish it.*

She looked up to the moon
hoping the night would show her
the art of love and home and finding her way;

She sat before the wildflowers
wishing for them to show her
the beauty of growing again;

She stood on mountain tops
believing that avalanches would teach her
the truth of letting go;

She laid beneath the evergreen
longing to overhear
the secrets of bearing all seasons;

She knew nothing,
but she was here,
she was here to learn.

She looked up to the *moon*
hoping the night would show her
the art of *love* and *home* and *finding her way*

And here in these lives we have built for ourselves,
shadows and cracks of what we once lived; here,
here live these hard and shivering moments;
but here I still am, *breathing, breathing, breathing* -
and none of this would seem real
if not for you
if not for your grace, your biding soul
that cast the light
towards the *good, good, good*
hiding in my shadows

it sounds like this

let me crawl inside and look around for any
interesting thing hanging about your heart

soul mates are more than just people;
but rather,
remedies for countless,
undefined afflictions of the soul

books,
and flowers,
and autumn leaves

a stranger's smile,
the morning coffee,
and something like freedom

but yes,
there is still you

she wants to believe they are laying under moonlight,
his eyes the stars, their bodies
two galaxies destined to meet
at a black hole, someday, somewhere

have you ever met a soul
who welcomed you like an old friend
even though your eyes had never met

a communion of sorts
unspoken and unknown before
but accompanied here as one and as whole

in this new territory
a bay of sorts
a threshold to keep you safe

a fixed point in an otherwise
unpredictable world

you, you, you

I couldn't decide if his eyes
solved all the mysteries of the world,

or created them

there's a rift between us,
do you feel it?

I think too easily and often we drift apart
like continents unforgiving of the initial break;
and now there are oceans that we cannot cross
despite our longing to come home

this is me,
saying I miss you

this is me,
wanting to find you again

there are different types of love, you know…

and it's devastating to know
that we don't always get to choose
which one someone gives us in return

blooming,
my heart may be,
yet I still fear the wake
you will leave in shadows
and empty sheets

I hear the skies ignite
when your lips meet mine

oh, allow me to get lost
        here, in the
        only place I want to stay -
                the heart of a man with
                a heart on his sleeve
                and a skipped beat for me

oh, allow me to get lost,
        the colors dancing in your eyes

tell me,
what is the greater risk:

to lose ourselves in everything we love, or
to lose ourselves because we never loved?

isn't it strange
how the very thing
that makes us feel most safe,
most alive

is the very thing
that breaks us the easiest?

it is terribly hard to look away from chaos,
and that's how our love worked;

we collided without intention
and we are still standing in the destruction

we are all cautionary tales

it is just a matter of finding
someone who is willing to risk the fall

rain soaked kisses
with *"just one more"*

shooting stars,
dawn's bliss,
afternoons of this -
you and I

a burning love
puts stars to shame,
blossoms the midnight flame

oh love,
we could paint the galaxies
with this type of love -
you and I

rain soaked kisses
with *"just one more"*

I have lived inside - so many
walls - and four don't make a
home - compared to your arms.

we cannot decide to love
we cannot compel anyone to love us
there is only love itself
and we are at its mercy
there's nothing we can do
but let it consume us
like a raging fire
through our parched bones

maybe we are made
of the same star dust,
maybe that's how
we found each other

we couldn't help ourselves
but be drawn to the same light
we felt within

she let him leaf through her;

like an old familiar story
he forgot he knew
and she longed to be

will you still love her
if she does not shine?

could you still pick her
from a night sky
if one day she stopped,
stopped burning so bright?

and could you show her
how to again?

yes, I believe in love;

he put it in my eyes,
my heart followed suit

we are all stories;
hidden within pages
of books along some shelf;

and often we don't get to choose
who leafs through,
touch like an old friend -
or tosses us aside
bored by page two;

but we all sit and wait
for the one who has been searching,
searching for a story told like ours

I think you're my tree,

and I pray autumn never comes

haiku 1

lights are always on
in your eyes they shine so bright;
can they guide me home?

are they real?

I am searching for that love
to shine a light in the darkness
when I forget that
monsters are not real

so many things depend on the
  strength of the wind,
  the depth of the ground,
  the presence of the fortress;

and I quickly learned, oh,
how could I sail,
how could I grow,
how could my heart *beat, beat, beat*
without *you, you, you*?

I have been told
that there are many
beautiful things
to be happy about -

you are all of them to me

this was love

a string of coincidences
gathering significance
becoming miracles

I used to stand before
mirrors and only
long to be something
else - now I stand
before your eyes
seeing what
I always missed

tell me about the wind,
how it bows the stems of the flowering blooms as if in prayer

tell me about the night,
how the vast infinity lays like a dark blanket for the stars

tell me about your heart,
how it stole breath from my lungs and still warmed my veins

can we hear a smile?

because I think even the wildflowers would pause for yours

because where one may stand - struck in awe -
of ten thousand red roses - one will seek - a so
subtle rain - and my love - I see both - when
your eyes find mine

thank you for loving me
when I was wild fire
without putting it out

thank you for loving me
when I was a hurricane
without taking shelter

thank you for loving me
when I was chaos
without trying to map it

then you'll turn to me,
and you'll ask
"how's your heart?"

you always know what gets me,
you always know what hides
behind that smile

you'll hold your eyes
right on mine,
and you'll hear me -
you'll hear the space,
the space between
these heart beats

your eyes whispering promises
deep into the pulse
and every part of me
will believe you

I'll always believe you

she wanted to be loved in pieces
because pieces were easier to reassemble
than an entire body
left behind in shambles;

but one piece at a time
he picked up what she left behind
and soon she would see,
that in his hands
she could never crumble

I used to hide behind only walls
but for once I'm not afraid
to let them go tumbling down
as long as you are here
standing on the inside
with your hand in mine
as they *fall, fall, fall*

you effortlessly occupy the silence
when words are few
and I cannot stand the stillness

solace

I find it in the night sky
and you find it in the ocean

you'd think we were destined
to never find each other
but don't forget
how the moon
controls the tides
and the sea
reflects the stars

and when you look at me
I swear the world isn't tired anymore
and the only place the sun is exploding
is in your eyes
and the last spark is *infinite*

my mind is its own galaxy
my heart a complicated constellation
that does not match its name
and you are the shooting star
it all stops and longs for

and when he wrapped me in his arms it was like
he was trying to hold all the broken pieces
together

and we fell
slowly
softly
and together into place

real love does not fill you,
it makes you want more
and that's the best kind of hunger

if I were to meet you at midnight
I think I would fall in love
because when the world is still
you can't help but feel your heart beat
you can't help but feel it leap from your chest
and into the only other living thing in such a
sleepy night

compare her to the ocean

because she is endless
and she will drown you
and you could never resist
her ravenous waves

there is a whole world inside her eyes, and he longed to spend his days traveling the lands and seas

sometimes
what we think is love
is merely
empty tangled sheets
and fear for what we gave away
in the name of wanting to be seen

this is a difference that takes
many nights to learn

if only we would learn to love
with the same energy we put in to trying to be loved

we spend years trying to define love
and even more years trying to find that love

and we miss it
we miss the love
in living and in being and in doing

we miss it because we tried to define
something that doesn't have a beginning
nor an end
but rather an existence,
an immeasurable existence

and the sooner we see that
the longer we get to enjoy
the truth,
the joy,
the grace,
of love
as love was always meant to be

she just wasn't the type of girl
you could read on a whim;
unsettled and calm all in one breath,
both roots and wings -
and when you try to tame
the fire in her ribs, maybe you will learn
that those feathered wings, her beating heart,
always preferred some chaos to play with

haiku 2

you burn away the
winter of this weary heart
bringing spring back home

and like a thief of my darkness
he became my shooting star

even the tiniest things mean so much

his hand on the small of her back
the extra stars in the black sky
a soft breeze to welcome the autumn
something good, something new
it all meant something
an existence not seen
in simple ways
but it all mattered
it all mattered

I wanted to know all the secrets to his thoughts
without him having to speak a word

you are a minefield
and I am standing at the edge
waiting for my destruction

you are one of the few
one of the rare
born of chaos and
remained untamed -
burning the world
with one color,
one color of you

do not fear struggling with love -
fear struggling with an empty heart

relationships are not bound by chains, but by
thousands of tiny threads that weave together
our mingling hearts

I don't know who I am
I don't think you do either
and maybe that's okay
maybe that's why we find each other;

to admire the uncertainty

you were born of chaos,
and it's not about finding
someone to tame it all;

wait for someone who learns to paint
with all these colors that pour
from your veins and soul

She sat before the *wildflowers*
wishing for them to show her
the beauty of *growing again*

it's okay to ask for help
it's okay to take off your wings
it's okay to let someone else carry you

your head and heart should be places you want to live in,
not run from

we control what we hold close,

and I don't think we ever learned
to exhale the things that break us

and she reminded herself
it was okay to be
unfinished

I think we often miss the people calling out to us
while we sit and pity ourselves for being alone

I once threw an old photo
off a merry go round
I watched as we turned
it turned itself about
faded corners mocking
the movement of
my following eyes

I wanted to throw more
but have you ever tried
to give up a memory
with the hopes that your
body would too forget?
because the merry go round stopped
and I'm standing above
a crumpled reminder
that I should have gone around
one more time

I think most of us are just Alice
and we learn to not speak
of our Wonderland and Haters

I once wanted to disappear

by once I mean daily,
daily I want to disappear;
step off the platform
that has been built
and called my life -
just for a moment,
a moment to not be - well, *this me*.
because often I believe
that I am not meant,
meant for this world; and really,
who of us are?

we are madness
we are beauty
we are all redemption
from the pieces

we have chaos in our hearts - but somehow -
tranquil - it beats - as if suspended from a flight
- we never fully landed from

at a young age we learned this art of hiding
of squeezing ourselves into corners and shadows
of quieting our voices and slowing our breath
and as we grew older we only got better

but tell me,
when did you stop asking,
asking to be found?

because hiding is too easy,
and maybe we stopped asking
because we hoped someone would come
despite our silent words

the moon - governess of tides moving - pale in peace - as she washes the air - painted by the black night does bring - and from such change of high and low - we see the seasons alter - as we do, too

repressed you

she marked the page -
a worn photograph.
always kept upside down
when she picked up where she left -
a hidden memory she didn't wish to share;

they say we repress our memories.
I wonder if we are just keeping
them safe somewhere
in the shadows - because no matter
how painful they are,
they are our most valuable
possessions; they make us
who we are

fall comes as the
most romantic of seasons,
as the leaves are falling
they're falling like
they're falling in love
with the ground

I am learning to appreciate - people for - their
ebb and flow - of change and moving along as
they come and go - like the seasons changing -
of bitter winter winds to fields of spring bloom
- a summer yellow glow into a crisp autumn
breath - I come to appreciate what I find in
each - knowing what once was - will always
come back - come back again

I long to feel
the silence of growing things;
the wildflowers who bloom
with no one to awe;
the big oak trembling
with no one to hear;
the peddles of a rose
falling alone;
the core of my bones,
the heat of my veins,
unknown beauty in the silence of life
that
keeps
going
on

oh, the world's remarkable capacity
to carry on
in every place
all at once;

all the world,
always going
somewhere

bowing in submission
to the summer storm

persistently poking their vibrancy
into the gray of the day

some may say
    when would they learn
    when would they fall

but those wildflowers
knew no such words

they would stay
    amidst the rubble
    the broken ways
    the shattered pieces
of wherever they chose

tell me something good
of the iridescent skies

tell me something calm
of the blooming fields

tell me something wild
of tangled hearts and breath

tell me something
of this vast infinity

do the flowers weep
not because their days are short
but rather ours
and they know all too well
how we do not stop enough
to gather them
in our hands
and hair
and bikes
and books
and eyes
and hearts

do they weep
for us, and
beg us to
stay, stay, stay

reverberation

we create these bonds -
people,
places,
moments;
misplaced by time,
connected in shadows;

millions of threads
weaving together
stolen pings;
heart strings tugging
for another
one
time
place;

always a force of light,
simplicity wrapped in
complexity;

I am grateful for those
connections,
those reverberations of
deep
heart
beats

I think nature wants to give
us something, too
the way it bends and
welcomes us as more than
shadows over roots
and leaves and petals
and death and life
and waiting and growing
and I think,
I think nature
wants us to notice
the beauty in what it so willingly
gives to us as just some passerby
of the willows and dandelions
and birch
and blades
and appreciate the silence
of growing things
because we too are silently growing
and soon we may forget
or be too old to see
or too stubborn to stop for
what nature wanted to give us
as an offering of peace
and solitude
and a not so lonely reminder
that life will always keep going on
and for that
there is no harm in slowing down
to admire a little dance
of wildflowers and roots
and cherries
and buds who just want you to say
it's okay

memories

a quiet murmur of long-forgotten
or simply untold
stories hung through the
warm night air
mixing with the laughter
and the voices
of the stories
being told;
right here
in familiar and new alike

like the rays of a rising sun
her heart unfurled
her body followed
allowing her to move on
from the darkness

of course it is easy
for us to love
the places where flower
already grow;
but I think we forget
that these places were once
just covered in dirt

maybe I'm too hopeful
but perhaps we could learn to love ourselves
when all we see is dirt
by remembering that one day
the flowers will grow

but we must be willing to love and admire
and water and cultivate
what is now just dirt

there is a crawl space within me
that no one can get to
and I swear the flood gates
are beating at the door
but I can't bear the weight
of drowning within myself
so I disguise the sound
with my still beating heart
and learn to dance
under the rhythm of destruction

anxiety

something like an internal asteroid

do not compare your immensities
to someone else's immensities
feel as deep as you must feel,
and do not add guilt to the list

we are just as strong as we assume fragile;
it is all a matter of which we choose to dance with

be disturbed

I think we're worse off
when we try to avoid the chaos

it is only when
we try and hide
that we find ourselves
going
under

all this time I could have been holding
the stars in my palms, twirling the galaxies
between my fingers
but I never learned to open my hands
in fear that the world would crush me

how many hands have tried to take mine in theirs
while I was too busy trying to make more room in my palms
for fear, and anxiety, and darkness

even if your symptoms sing a familiar tune,
your feelings will always be different wavelengths,
learn to listen to the rhythms and you'll come to learn
that they play so well together

treating anxiety feels like
pulling back the green curtain
that reveals the true Oz -
with the hope that
we can still make
our way back home
from this horrible dream

my imprint remains as the flowers grow around me
at least something with life is growing
while I'm slowly fading

my own mind is at odds with me
all it wants is to dance in the midnight
but when the sun comes up it runs and hides

don't take a wrecking ball to your own heart
before the world gets to hear its tune

a pause amid the hum of thoughts

this is my soul and the world unwinding,
this is my heart in the still winter air,
this is coming home

I'd like to remember this

remember,
daily the world
will emerge as it pleases

so who are we
to expect the sun to rise
and reveal a day
the same as before

who are we
to ask so much
when we too
refuse to stay the same

the sky is always singing
and I think we stopped listening

I think endings are lies
tell me when did we start thinking that we had some sort of limit
some sort of full that still left us empty when life reached its "end"
tell me why can't tomorrow surprise us just once more
you know, I bet we could be so full that we could not bear,
but then the sun rises and we cannot help but linger,
thirst for its warmth,
for *more, more, more*
I promise that there is more to remember
even when we have been told that life is already too full
and we are at its "end"

don't be afraid to find your way by moonlight
while everyone is waiting for the sunrise

everybody has a story to tell

we just have to remember
that the best parts of them are not skin and bone

you must exhale in order to create space to inhale

it has been one hell of a year,
one hell of a life;
I have worn the season like a scar,
felt the pain deep in the bags under
my eyes, running down
over my cheeks;
I weathered all these midnights,
fought for these dawns

this
this is what surviving looks like,
my dear;
it looks a lot like *falling*,
falling to pieces,
crumbling,
shaking -
overcoming

do not underestimate the transition
between farewell and new departure;

take your time -
you hurt,
then you heal

I will stop counting my breaths,
I will let my heart beat free,
I will allow my mind to wander;
one day I will feel these things
without fear of being suffocated
by the very breath, beat, and thought

a bird inside her heart
wings that flutter with each new breath
movement that dances

and I can see it in her eyes
with each beat
its finding the wind

now watch her fly

I want to find in today what will make this moment
significant in the simplest joys of subatomic this and that
and maybe one or two untethering pleasures
of light and joy and simple living

like the wildflowers

so when you are broken
and tossed into the wind
remember it is possible
to grow yourself again

what doesn't kill you makes you stronger

but sometimes what doesn't kill us still destroys us

and sometimes it is hard to say no to the very thing destroying us
when that very thing makes the world say
"*come, we accept you*"

from the inside we crumble, crumble, crumble
with every word, every look, every lie

so do not tell me that I'm not dying just because my body
still moves when you say move

take care of your body
if not before
than now

take care of your body
not to prepare her to be handed out
but to prepare her to house you

take care of your heart
if not before
than now

take care of your heart
not to toughen him up for the break
but to strengthen him to beat for you, you, you

take care of your mind
if not before
than now

take care of your mind
not to silence the darkness
but to feed it with warmth of who you are

She stood on *mountain* tops
believing that avalanches would teach her
the truth of *letting go*

you have to learn to let it go
or the tears you keep locked away
the pain you hold for far too long
will turn you into stone
from the inside out

we break from the inside out
and our cries are muffled
by the world's applause
for the smile we perfected

it chips away
layer by layer
from within
and no one can see
how brittle we have become
until at last they reach to pull us home
only to grasp dust in their palms

do not make your body a war zone

we are capable of conjuring all kinds of gaps;
and far too often
I think we make them
with our veins
turning our mind
against our heart
and our words
against our soul

I will find you when you are not here;
in everything that was within you
in everything that you manifested into

I will find your essence
because who you are, what you are made of
does not die away

remember this

when someone leaves
we are allowed to welcome another
but they do not take their place,
they take their own place

that is the beauty;
that we will always carry the ones who left
with us
not because we are weak
but because they keep us whole
and if we try to cast them off
then surely we will fall to pieces

they won't always choose us -
a heavy dust to shake
from these bones

oh, but we move along -
our worth a hue
of how we still *breathe, breathe, breathe*

let their leaving wake
leave us only thankful
that the world still keeps us in mind
and that somewhere
someone is saying *"hello"*
and soon so shall we

my skin will forget,
it is science, but the heart
doesn't work that way

our hearts are not old sweaters
so do not try and stretch out the corners
just to accommodate someone
you are not meant to fit

we are far too young
and I don't want to believe in
the unraveling of our existence
in that marked temporary

we are far too young and
this pain is surely
the night before the dawn

we are far too young to believe
a loosening of nerves and love
is the ending of ourselves

as if allowing
our pounding heart
a chance to say:
See?
I loved enough to lose,
I felt enough to weep;

but I think we stop listening
before we get the chance to hear
the last whispering of:
now let's keep on

we are far too young
and this is just today

I may disappear into shadows and corners
of my mind and of this world
but I never asked you not to find me
I never wanted to leave you behind

and did I mention
that daily I still look for you
hoping you will finally look for me
in the shadows and the corners
because daily you just pass me by
and I think you forget
that I belong in this world, too

we are something someone lost along the way,
and I am not sure if that is pleasing or
obliterating

this is her heart now;
smoldering to pieces
of what she thought was love
but you are walking away -

this is your doing;
this is what happens
when you light a spark
just to watch it burn

there are stars in the eyes of a boy I once knew
and I long to know who they are leading home
tonight

I'm always missing the wrong people

aching for the
imprint of
yesterday
to be filled
by something
not of you

but we all know
I am always
missing
the wrong people;
and I have found
a home in this
muscle memory
of you,
here in the pain
I have welcomed -
and I will let
you stay
in this wake you left,
ache and all
ache and all
ache and all
I will let you stay

I have more *sorrys* to udder than
a blossoming meadow - only -
they feel more like a trench of
thorn covered roses

you just don't silence beauty

she told me all she wanted was to be heard - that
shook my bones - because it meant she had started
- to silence beauty

feeling the weight - of all who wished her silent -
a far too young soul - to have to wish - to just be
heard

haiku 3

a somber morning
a heart bids ado to a
love it once knew

haiku 4

loss has taught me that
the world will spin even when
you beg to get off

the love we lose

I wanted so badly
to have something
that was never
even mine to miss;

and that is all I know -
the longing it left me with

when they left
they took a piece -

but they did not lessen you

I heard someone once say
that we love something stronger
when we learn to miss it;

but I think I turned cold
sometime along the way
because you are still gone
and I cannot bare to hear

the end of our story
the end of our story
the end of our story

if I learned anything the hard way
it is this -

feel safe in your own skin
before you try and crawl into someone else's

in times of sorrow - as grief ebbs and flows - as I reach for your hand - to find empty air - I will remember the way - you reached for mine - when you were still here - and my heart still whole we always knew silence was deafening, but we never knew its power to shake our bones out of rest - we never knew silence like we did that night the darkness called tears to the surface and heart beats shallow - the silence broke us to the core, breaking loose everything we tried to hide - and no matter how deep the wound it showed us, we are better off once we face its deafening song

I once believed
sadness a color
that ran through my veins
that tangled my hair;
I once welcomed
grief as a longtime friend
to weigh on my bones
to beat in my heart -

and all along
I longed for someone to say
"*oh, my dear*
grief is not your color"

to the father I knew

we do not get a map of grief,
we do not get the answers;
but when an eleven-year-old girl loses the man
who gave her laughter and joy and love,
she comes to learn:

grief is a dance
only you can learn
a familiar tune
only you can hear
of heartbeat and memory
of a joy it was
to love and build
what you may now only miss

now here I stand,
and I have lived half my life without you,
and I will love you my whole life long
in this dance that is forever ours

so keep sending me the stars,
keep kissing the wildflowers;
I know you're still making
this laughter and joy and love

grief is not sorrow

I have found no place for sorrow - I have no hope for grief to be - anything but the ebb and flow - of your heartbeat - still running through my bones

now wrapped in your old shirt - I will only cry in joy - of these memories - these memories that you left

the birds were sadly
singing a song
of a familiar tune I once knew
and when I asked
them to sing it again
they just sang your name
they sang your name
they sang your name

loving on

grief does something to us:
it wrecks us,
but with the intention of allowing us
to discover the importance
of loving on

and more importantly,
that we are not alone in our suffering
nor in our loving on

dear daddy,

you left mid-sentence
and I have spent my entire life
trying to piece together
what you wanted me to hear

did you look her in the eyes?
did you see
the gray of rain-laden storm clouds,
wide, wild, turbulent…

did you see the remains,
the scorch of the fire
you let burn
before walking away?

this was you;
it's all in her eyes;
do you see it?

the ocean does not sleep
and maybe that is why we run to it
to cast off our sleepless worries and fears

I dare the stars to let me outlast them - but then
what would I be - a girl lost in the sea of black
nights - with no north

I cannot bear the thought - so I will keep on
counting the stars - and let them
stay, stay, stay

do not be hustled out of pain you earned

barren trees

now I see a still reminder of what fighting looks like:
emptiness

depression rips you apart from the inside -
cell by cell by vein by vein
turning your bones against each other

I know,
because I am still trying to teach mine not to destroy each other

what I learned about depression

it is not an explosion
wiping out all light

but more of a slow, silent
cascading of shifting foundation
with the lights occasionally flickering in response

which is far worse than any blackout,
because the lights just flicker
like our weakened hope
and we know,
we know neither will stay

the inevitable low

to weigh as much as the ocean
sucked into that wave you hope never finds you
the one that takes you under
takes your breath
disorients you completely
and never brings you back to the surface

what me and books have in common

worn pages
creased corners
fading spine

something keeps chiseling away at me
deep inside
maybe in my soul
maybe just my bones
but I feel each piece
crumbling
and maybe that is why I wear so much armor
so many layers
because I cannot imagine the destruction
of falling apart from the inside out
of my soul actually falling apart
before busting from my chest

against, against, against

depression settles like a shadow over your body while you sleep and it mutes every frequency into blankness into fog

everyone thinks you cannot laugh but I could not cry
because I could not feel my way through the body
that was supposed to belong to me

her trust was the hardest thing to give
because like the worn beach
she trusted the tide
only for the waves to come back
and try to break her earth

a sea made of tears from lost lovers, but I think
most of the tears are for the love never known

some days the heart of every living thing
is beating inside my chest;
other days I am a barren desert

do not try and take away the pain - because pain is not always a burden - but a way - a way through what we thought would destroy us - what we thought was the end - but pain often knows the way to the light

we are infinitely more prepared
to forget their voice
than we are their presence

haiku 5

I feel like tired
eyes with an absence of who
I once used to be

people are not good hiding places
because at some point
that hiding place
will need to hide itself

does the moon weep - for strangers who do not see - that they are not alone - in the darkness that they fear - hoping the light of its full - will bring one home - to the arms of another - before the dawn - sends them away the clock does not move any slower, and yet there are moments when I swear I am moving faster than light and time cannot keep up, and then there comes the descent, and time does not seem to want to move at all

I am my own black hole, perfecting the skill of
simultaneously sucking me deeper into myself and pushing
away the rest of existence;

it allows me life in the form of burning stars circling the
darkness and a dull hum of hope but not without a chaotic
battle of my strongest wills

my mood does not reflect that which sits
perched at my window sill
I am inside out
and every part of me is trembling

medication does not fix - it rearranges and
gathers the highs and lows into a flat
lined beat and we must learn how to adjust the flow
from then on out - and there is a reason why
fighting becomes harder than settling with the
once before chaos

I think the memories
will keep fading
but there is this place
a place the wind
will always blow
a place deep within
within my chest
and through a hole
I cannot mend
a hole that sings,
still sings your name

why we pull ourselves apart

be big enough to be visible when sought
but small, quiet, accepting
hide well
learn to shrink when they turn away from you
but never be too far away
master the art of fitting in
but stand out just enough to not be forgotten
forgotten is lonely
but do not want
be available for wanting
do not want

we don't get back the nights
we decided to say yes to feel *better, better, better*

instead we are left with mornings
that left us *smaller, smaller, smaller*

I sought out love
in ways I knew would be accepted
I said yes with my body
when my mind cried no
I sought after the darkness
knowing the dawn would leave me numb
I made myself small, quiet, and agreeable
I gave and gave and gave,
gave pieces of myself away
in hopes that someday
someone would not accept
anything less than all of me
but now I only fear
that there is not enough of me
to give *whole*

we hold on to memories
because in those memories
we can stop whenever we want
we can freeze the moment
and make it infinite in perfection and stillness
even if the moment that comes next is finite and crushing

the baby I never knew

tell me,
how do we recover
when we have been broken
from the inside
a brokenness that
never reached the surface
never had a chance to breathe,
to heal

how do we survive
when our lungs stopped trying
to inhale, exhale, keep us alive
how do we come back
when our body has betrayed us
how do we come back
when we are less than what we started with
tell me, please
because I am still breaking
empty, empty, empty

part of your soul is an indestructible, brilliant diamond
and after a long day of trying to wreck yourself
I hope you finally realize that diamonds are born
from fallen star dust
and you cannot destroy the infinite night sky

She laid beneath the *evergreen*
longing to overhear
the secrets of *bearing all seasons*

I wish we felt more strongly for real people
but I think our attention is too small
and we are always choosing the temporary
and people are not temporary

anxiety comes like the
wayfarers trod
to the wildflowers stem;
sudden and fierce

the wildflower
stubborn and worn
will sway again -

a wildflower
free and unstrained
knows their strength
with few to see
the beauty that paints yellow fields
and purple patches
singing through the silence

they do not weep
when the wayfarers leave
for soon they will rebuild
from the wake they left
as all that is lost
is once again found

you, too,
will rebuild
will rebuild
will rebuild

the world suffers while you are hiding
the world would suffer if you left

but when you are here, the world is whole

whatever you have been traveling from
wherever you hope to go
you are here now
and that's a good ending and beginning

sometimes people need us to be their
map, and sometimes people need us to be
a lit front porch welcoming them home
when they find their own way -

sometimes we need
to hand out maps,
and sometimes we need
to hand out grace

no matter - we need to be
safe places to land

I tell you you can
and I know you will whisper
but what if I can't?

and I just hope one day
this voice of mine is louder
than what you have been shaped to tell yourself

there will always be people we are meant to meet
and those people we do not meet
are still meant to exist
because each of us
is holding a map
and we are all meant to cross the paths
of the people who need it most

this world is delicate
and maybe we do not know it
but if just one
just one of us was not
then this world would be different;
turned a degree or two the other way
all because there was not
just one of us as we should be;
so stay -
stay and keep this world where it should be
the degree where it is
the density as it should
because the world will know
and we will see in the shadows
of what has changed
of what should not have changed -
so stay

you will bleed beauty dry
by trying to find the source
until you realize the beauty
is in simply living,
and you missed your own
by trying to find some answer
some key to this mystery

quiet your anxious heart,
let loose that tangled trance;

leave your weary bones behind,
let us learn the slow dance

don't give people
so much power over you
that their
silence
leaves you questioning
your worth

there are a million lives that do not know me - millions more I cannot know - how do we go on - bound to be mere strangers in the night - collapsing - in our own longing - for someone to tell us - just who we are note to passerby: *"please read on, do not burn me yet"*

you are weakness,
and you are greatness;
all wrapped up in one
masterpiece of life
blessed with loveliness

"dreamers will always crash back to earth"

but I'm not ready - to bid the moon - a sorrowful adieu - for there are stars that hold me - and there are galaxies all tangled in my hair

so I think I will stay - I will stay up here among the tides - of those dreamers who left too soon

the horizon's glow - bowing for
the wildflowers
perched at its edge - yellows,
purples, reds -
mirroring the sun's setting dance -
all right here, here for you

don't be afraid
to burst into bloom,
it's all just hope
trying to come
to the light

slowly
softly
I fall in love
with the possibility
of subtle beauty

lost in the show
a leaf gone falling free
finally learned that
letting go meant
falling in love

slowly
softly
every moment learned
to be its own
worthy beauty

a cure for anxiety is not a simple matter, but I
have learned that a breath of fresh air on a late
Sunday morning in Spring will subside the ache

your eyes
tell a
tale of
a story
that kept

going.

we are creatures of hiding
but as we whisper
"here I am"
into the crack of
darkness hiding us
our even deeper
need is revealed
as we long to be *found*

I think we appreciate the slow drift
of a loosely letting go leaf
because we ourselves fall so quickly,
painfully even,
but this drift of the leaf
and the snowflake alike
make falling look pleasant,
or even necessary

look at us:
fighting against ourselves
while begging for the world to be at peace

sure,
some people feel the weight
of everything they are not

but I think
we also bear
guilt for everything we *are*

but the bird does not need
a reason to spread its wings and fly
nor does it need a reason to perch for quite some time

a miracle we may call - anything we manage to save from history - so let me steal this moment - lost in mundane - let me hold it deep within my beating chest - so time may not take - the way the wind worked with the sun - and the flowers seemed to dance to a song - only they could hear

there is a new thing
here in the dawn

the old is not lost
but soon we will see
how
like the seasons
what once was
always comes back

not the same
as we never are

the colors remain
but the new is still new
mixed with the lost
to remind us
we are always
moving on

like when the winter white
hugs the autumn leaf in
and the summer heat
grabs the yellow spring tight

built on what has passed
anew may only abound
when the old is seen
when the old is praised to a tune
to the welcome of something new

your current storm does not define you,
nor does it confine you

winter comes like a barren blanket - to cover a bed - of unnamed color - but what is made all white - will soon welcome in - the fields of yellow bloom - to bring in a fiery red summer - to fall softly with autumn's embrace - and alas - winter shall throw itself again - regain its rightful place - as new can only come - with the bend to - the seasons of four

and I am nostalgic for - seasons yet to come - but we must pass through - must walk in - each as they come - because we must - we can - we should - find ourselves - anew in each

maybe healing
does not look like putting all the pieces
back where we found them;

maybe we were never
meant to be the same; maybe
we can move forward, different than
when we fell

is your hope true,
or do you simply keep looking out of habit?

I think it is important to know the difference

white as snow

we were

beaten down,
abused,
by the words of a world
that does not even know our name

we are

raised up,
redeemed,
by the innocent blood
of a Savior who gives us new life

the days do not stop and no one gets
more seconds in a minute and the only way
to stretch a moment is to stop counting
and l*ive, live, live*

I want to be - or maybe I am looking for - a
vessel - of sorts

could I be the ship - that guides a soul - to a
harbored dawn

or maybe it is me - unknowingly - lost at sea -
looking for something to be - some beacon of
hope

or maybe - maybe we are all searching

and - maybe we do not see - the vessel we need
- is the vessel we are

after all - who else but me - knows the way
home

have you ever seen a night so pure and blanketed with relief that you could step off the side of a cliff and float among the stars as they sucked you in and reduced your gravity to be among them for just a moment before the moon gently placed your feet back on the ground like the moving tides

I wonder who gets to hear our wishes and
secrets and regrets and fears and dreams when
we whisper them to the sea and the waves
refuse to give them back;

I wonder who is listening across the way maybe
just the man on the moon or maybe a lost soul
with a seashell to her ear;

Perhaps that is how and why we feel so
connected with the sea because we always know
someone will find us when they need us most
and we most need to be heard.

I want to stay here until the last possible
moment until the shadows steal my breath
again and fade my smile

I want to stay here until the light is so dim my
eyes can barely bare to squint again

I just want to stay here and feel - I want to feel

the world is watching and
I am trying not to crumble
the world is listening and
I am trying not to shake

but it's this world,
this world that makes
me crumble and shake

no wonder people wander
to disappear
no wonder people long
for the earth to swallow them up

I don't want the world to watch
I don't want the world to listen

I just want to stand here
and be okay

we are all lost
and I don't think any of us
are actually looking for another way

we wear the chaos too well

anchor us in the steady and true,
          lead us back, always back to You

love, let love mend us in Your truth
strip, strip us of ourselves for You
root, root us in Your grace

anchor us upon the power and peace,
          bring us back, always back to you

I am so frail

but I think my bones are still hoping
to find their way back again

I am still trying to conquer the mountains of my own body

and I am finally starting to understand the importance of maps

we all feel the need to move towards light
whether in the stars or someone's eyes
and sometimes the light is finite
fading as we quickly lose grip
and sometimes we swear the world is infinite in the glow
and we pray we will never have to fear the shadows

we are all our own parallel universes;

structured and chaotic
beautiful and strange

God keeps giving us people
because He is not done telling us a story

I want to hold the stars
before they are only dust

maybe that is all we want, too -
to be seen before we are only
lingering light and reminders
of what we once were
of what we once tried to be

whenever you feel lost
remember that you are a home
to your own heartbeat

look straight up -
do you ever image what's out there?
do you ever feel like it will ever just collapse on you?
I think we would be better off among the debris

sometimes attics hold thousands of forgotten memories and sometimes they contain the corners of the universe waiting for us to discover their existence; or maybe it is all the same - I think the choice is in what we choose to seek and what we choose to hide from

beneath the sunken eyes and deep set pain there
is still a fog of something that longs to be pulled
into focus

of joy, joy, joy

everything bright needed to be refined;
so allow me my chaos

I have seen the strength you cry for -
it lives inside of you
my dear, behind the fear and dusty hope…

and this is your reminder.

for every day, every journey, every unknown

can You lead me where I cannot go alone,
could You take me deep to the unknown,
will You light this path I tend to fear?

wherever I wander, let it be with You;
on this journey I embark,
forever I promise,
with a desire to go for You.

Lord bind my very heart,
in all that I am, all that I do,
root me to You

I have a lust for places I have never been
for moments I have never felt

I have a longing for scenes I have yet to see
and horizons I will not believe

I have a desire to be amongst the unknown,
the journey where only dreams can be true

God given

two arms around me as heaven surrounds me
hope that saved me and grace that gave me
a way to come home, a way to see again

a heart believed and a new soul received
with faith that grounds me and a great love around me
heaven has blessed this life with great mercy

I tend to put my pain in a box
in hopes that sheltering it will keep it contained
but I have come to learn
that there is no small when it comes to falling apart
there is no hiding

we must face the monsters
we must face the monsters

because hiding the pain gives power to the source
while we slowly lose ourselves more, more, more
and here is the truth I am finally seeing
we do not get to live
until we face what has tried to kills us
because we have not conquered anything
by stuffing it in corners of darkness and shame

we must face the monsters
we must face the monsters

may you find laughter in the midst of broken days

I want you to listen to the whispers of your wildest dreams
I want to see the shine in your eyes as you set them free
I want you to shake up this world

I want you to dream big
so big the world laughs;
find your way by moonlight while they search
empty in the daylight

paint in the stars
make it shine
make the world stop
make them wonder

I want you to live it and breathe it
never afraid to stand alone
and fill it with a bit of lost hope and wrong turns
just so you don't forget that dreams
are never perfect

I want you to move and shake the world's mold
I want you to dare to live it every day
as the world stares

show them what real dreams are
show them what it is like to keep the wild
show them that dreams worth living
are not marked by boundaries

no guidelines or limitations
no fine print or second edition
written in ink on your very soul
this is your story, and you must tell it

show them that you are a dreamer
and make them believe that they are too
because this world needs more believers,
more world shakers, movers and boundary breaker
this world needs more hearts ablaze for something more,
more than just day-to-day
this world needs more wild, relentless, and
crazy dreamers like you

this world needs eyes that see beyond what the rest
stay fixed upon
past the fog and up into the mountains
after the sunset and into the moonlight
beyond the comfort of the world, and into
the wonder

the rest of the world will stand still, overcome by
the shouts of conformity
but you, my little dreamer, are free

She knew nothing,
but she was here,
she was here to *learn*.

Katherine Henson, penning as k.e., lives in small town Illinois where she spends her days as an avid coffee drinker. This is her first self-published book. Day-to-day she is a barista, business owner, freelance writer and designer, and social media guru. Katherine has been writing for as long as she can remember, and it is both her love language and preferred choice of communication. For Katherine, writing has been a way to escape and discover; through body image issues, depression, anxiety, and loss Katherine has used her words as a way to be honest with herself, while also helping others understand that they are not alone.

She graduated from Olivet Nazarene University in 2015 with a degree in Criminal Justice and Social Work and plans to return for her Masters (in what she does not know). She owns her own coffee business (mycoffeeism.com), and has high hopes of opening her own coffee shop and bookstore one day. She also has three tattoos and feels like that's an important thing to note.

Follow Katherine Henson

Twitter: @kehnsn
Instagram: @kehnsn
Facebook: /kehnsn
Tumblr: katherinehenson
Blog: katherinehenson.com